I'D RATHER BE

AT THE CABIN

Paintings by

DEBBIE CRABTREE

HARVEST HOUSE PUBLISHERS

EUGENE, OREGON

I'd Rather Be at the Cabin

Copyright © 2004 by Harvest House Publishers
Published by Harvest House Publishers
Eugene, Oregon 97402
www.harvesthousepublishers.com

ISBN 0-7369-1306-8

Artwork is copyrighted © by Debbie Crabtree. This is a licensed product with permission from Sagebrush Fine Art. For more information regarding art prints featured in this book, please contact:

Sagebrush Fine Art
   3065 S. West Temple
   Salt Lake City, UT 84115
   800.643.7243
www.sagebrushfineart.com

Design and production by Garborg Design Works, Minneapolis, Minnesota.

Harvest House Publishers has made every effort to trace the ownership of all poems and quotes. In the event of a question arising from the use of a poem or quote, we regret any error made and will be pleased to make the necessary correction in future editions of this book.

Scripture quotations are taken from the Holy Bible, New International Version®, Copyright © 1973, 1978, 1984 by the International Bible Society. Used by permission of Zondervan Publishing House. All rights reserved.

Printed in China

05 06 07 08 09 10 / LP / 10 9 8 7 6 5 4 3 2

Nothing is more beautiful than the loveliness of the woods before sunrise.

GEORGE WASHINGTON CARVER

3

After endless days of commuting on the freeway to an antiseptic, sealed-window office, there is a great urge to backpack in the woods and build a fire.

CHARLES KRAUTHAMMER

I love any discourse of rivers,

I went to the woods because I wished to live deliberately, to front only
the essential facts of life, and see if I could not learn what it had to
teach, and not, when I came to die, discover that I had not lived.

HENRY DAVID THOREAU

and fish, and fishing.

IZAAK WALTON

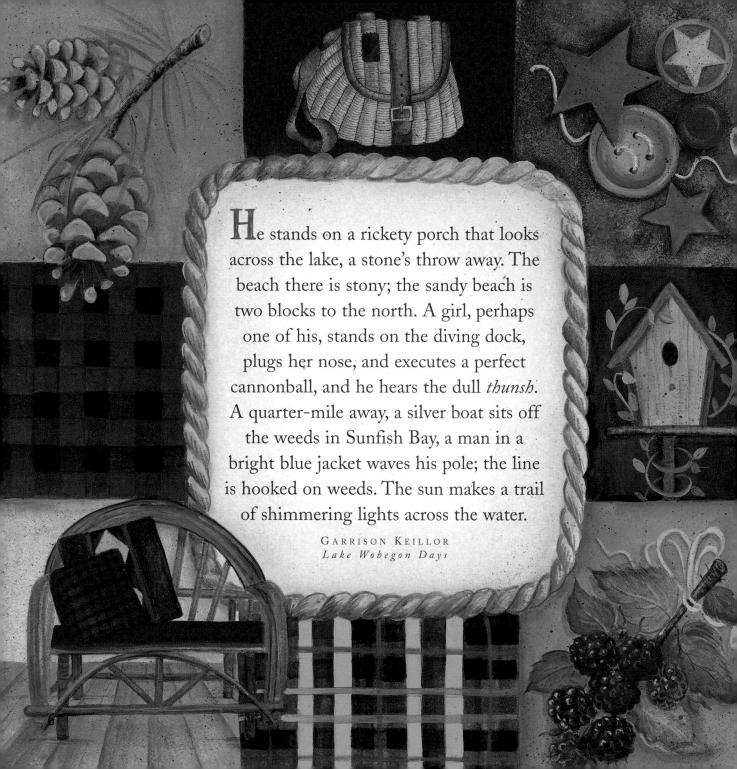

He stands on a rickety porch that looks across the lake, a stone's throw away. The beach there is stony; the sandy beach is two blocks to the north. A girl, perhaps one of his, stands on the diving dock, plugs her nose, and executes a perfect cannonball, and he hears the dull *thunsh*. A quarter-mile away, a silver boat sits off the weeds in Sunfish Bay, a man in a bright blue jacket waves his pole; the line is hooked on weeds. The sun makes a trail of shimmering lights across the water.

GARRISON KEILLOR
Lake Wobegon Days

This is the meeting place where God has set his bounds. Here is enough, at last, for eye and thought, restful and satisfying and illimitable. Here rest is sweet, and the picture of it goes with us on our homeward way, more lasting in memory than the sunset on the meadows or the lingering light across the silent stream.

ISAAC OGDEN RANKIN

The woods are lovely, dark, and deep,
But I have promises to keep,
And miles to go before I sleep,
And miles to go before I sleep.

ROBERT FROST

Time to put off the world and go somewhere and find my health again in the search.

W. B. YEATS

If solid happiness we prize,
Within our breast this jewel lies,
And they are fools who roam.
The world has nothing to bestow;
From our own selves our joys must flow,
And that dear hut, our home.

NATHANIEL COTTON

We went straight to the cabin of the game warden, Uncle Jim Owens; and he instantly accepted us as his guests, treated us as such, and accompanied us throughout our fortnight's stay north of the river. A kinder host and better companion in a wild country could not be found.

THEODORE ROOSEVELT

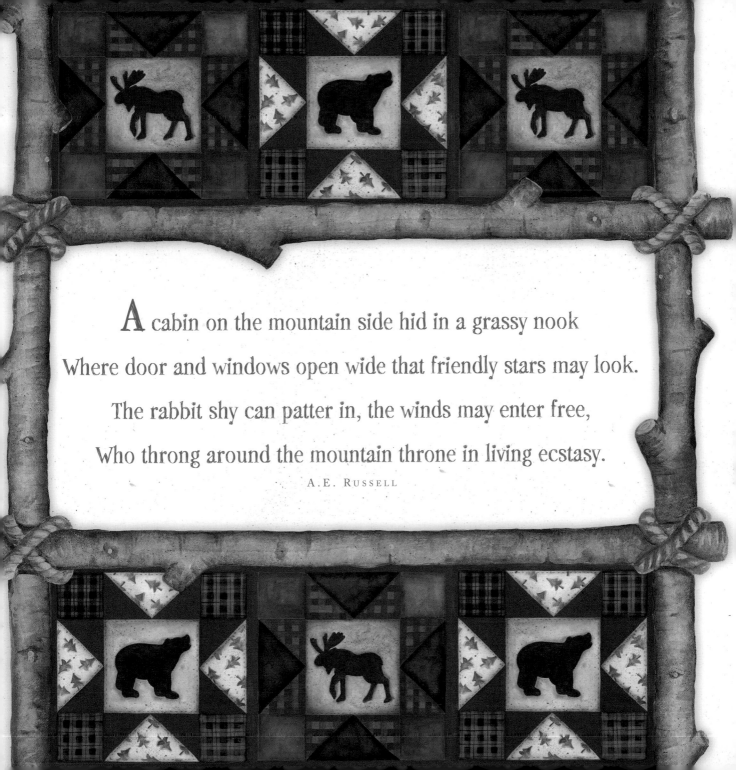

A cabin on the mountain side hid in a grassy nook

Where door and windows open wide that friendly stars may look.

The rabbit shy can patter in, the winds may enter free,

Who throng around the mountain throne in living ecstasy.

A. E. RUSSELL

The voices of the subterranean
river in the shadows were different
from the voices of the sunlit river ahead.
In the shadows against the cliff the river was
deep and engaged in profundities, circling back
on itself now and then to say things over to be sure
it had understood itself. But the river ahead came
out into the sunny world like a chatterbox, doing
its best to be friendly. It bowed to one shore and then
to the other so nothing would feel neglected.

NORMAN MACLEAN
A River Runs Through It

Rock Creek was as wild as the Rocky Mountains. Here and there a...log cabin alone disturbed the dogwood and the judas-tree, the azalea and the laurel. The tulip and the chestnut gave no sense of struggle against a stingy nature. The soft, full outlines of the landscape carried no hidden horror of glaciers in its bosom. The brooding heat of the profligate vegetation; the cool charm of the running water; the terrific splendor of the June thunder-gust in the deep and solitary woods, were all sensual, animal, elemental.

HENRY ADAMS

A noise like of a hidden brook
In the leafy month of June,
That to the sleeping woods all night
Singeth a quiet tune.

SAMUEL TAYLOR COLERIDGE

13

We walked in so pure and
bright a light, gilding the
withered grass and leaves,
so softly and serenely bright,
I thought I had never bathed
in such golden flood, without
a ripple or a murmur to it.
The west side of every wood
and rising ground gleamed
like the boundary of Elysium,
and the sun on our backs
seemed like a gentle
herdsman driving us
home at evening.

HENRY DAVID THOREAU

By the time he had reached the cabin, a matter of some thirty or forty good paces, the water no longer splashed from his pail, for a thin film of ice prevented it. Rea stood fifteen feet from the cabin, his back to the wind, and threw the water. Some of it froze in the air, most of it froze on the logs. The simple plan of the trapper to incase the cabin with ice was easily divined. All day the men worked, easing only when the cabin resembled a glistening mound. It had not a sharp corner nor a crevice. Inside it was warm and snug, and as light as when the chinks were open.

ZANE GREY
The Last of the Plainsmen

15

They cleared the bank with a rush, swung to the left, and dashed up to a small log cabin. It was a deserted cabin of a single room, eight feet by ten on the inside. Messner unharnessed the animals, unloaded his sled and took possession. The last chance wayfarer had left a supply of firewood. Messner set up his light sheet-iron stove and started a fire. He put five sun-cured salmon into the oven to thaw out for the dogs, and from the water-hole filled his coffee-pot and cooking-pail.

While waiting for the water to boil, he held his face over the stove. The moisture from his breath had collected on his beard and frozen into a great mass of ice, and this he proceeded to thaw out. As it melted and dropped upon the stove it sizzled and rose about him in steam. He helped the process with his fingers, working loose small ice-chunks that fell rattling to the floor.

JACK LONDON
A Day's Lodging

Rank jewel flower poured gold from dainty cornucopias and lavender beard-tongue offered honey to a million bumbling bees; water smart-weed spread a glowing pink background, and twining amber dodder topped the marsh in lacy mist with its delicate white bloom. Straight before them a white-sanded road climbed to the bridge and up a gentle hill between the young hedge of small trees and bushes, where again flowers and bright colours rioted and led to the cabin yet invisible. On the right, the hill, crowned with gigantic forest trees, sloped to the lake; midway the building stood, and from it, among scattering trees all the way to the water's edge, were immense beds of vivid colour. Like a scarf of gold flung across the face of earth waved the misty saffron, and beside the road running down the hill, in a sunny, open space arose tree-like specimens of thrifty magenta pokeberry.

GENE STRATTON-PORTER
The Harvester

fireside happiness, to hours of ease
Blest with that charm, the certainty to please.
SAMUEL ROGERS

To me a lush carpet of pine needles or spongy grass is more welcome than the most luxurious Persian rug.

HELEN KELLER

There was little of the dampness of the virgin woods; and the morning air, though cool, as is ever the case, even in midsummer, in regions still covered with trees, was balmy; and, at that particular spot, it came to the senses of le Bourdon loaded with the sweets of many a wide glade of his favorite white clover. Of course, he had placed his cabin near those spots where the insect he sought most abounded; and a fragrant site it proved to be, in favorable conditions of the atmosphere. Ben had a taste for all the natural advantages of his abode, and was standing in enjoyment of its placid beauties...

JAMES FENIMORE COOPER
Oak Openings

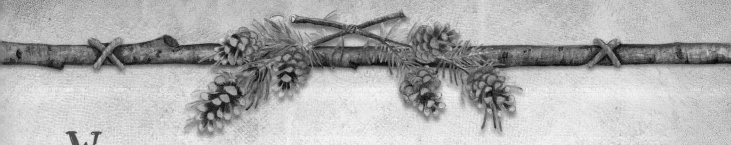

When I first took up my abode in the woods, that is, began to spend my nights as well as days there, which, by accident, was on Independence Day, or the Fourth of July, 1845, my house was not finished for winter, but was merely a defence against the rain, without plastering or chimney, the walls being of rough, weather-stained boards, with wide chinks, which made it cool at night. The upright white hewn studs and freshly planed door and window casings gave it a clean and airy look, especially in the morning, when its timbers were saturated with dew, so that I fancied that by noon some sweet gum would exude from them. To my imagination it retained throughout the day more or less of this auroral character, reminding me of a certain house on a mountain which I had visited a year before. This was an airy and unplastered cabin, fit to entertain a travelling god, and where a goddess might trail her garments. The winds which passed over my dwelling were such as sweep over the ridges of mountains, bearing the broken strains, or celestial parts only, of terrestrial music. The morning wind forever blows, the poem of creation is uninterrupted; but few are the ears that hear it. Olympus is but the outside of the earth everywhere.

HENRY DAVID THOREAU

He alone stretches out the heavens
and treads on the waves of the sea.
He is the Maker of the Bear and
Orion, the Pleiades and the
constellations of the south.
He performs wonders that
cannot be fathomed, miracles
that cannot be counted.

THE BOOK OF JOB

My heart is awed within me
when I think of the great miracle
that still goes on, in silence,
round me—the perpetual
work of thy creation, finished,
yet renewed forever. Written
on thy works I read the lesson
of thy own eternity.

WILLIAM CULLEN BRYANT

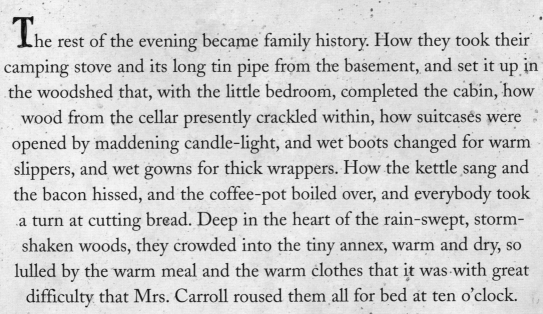

The rest of the evening became family history. How they took their camping stove and its long tin pipe from the basement, and set it up in the woodshed that, with the little bedroom, completed the cabin, how wood from the cellar presently crackled within, how suitcases were opened by maddening candle-light, and wet boots changed for warm slippers, and wet gowns for thick wrappers. How the kettle sang and the bacon hissed, and the coffee-pot boiled over, and everybody took a turn at cutting bread. Deep in the heart of the rain-swept, storm-shaken woods, they crowded into the tiny annex, warm and dry, so lulled by the warm meal and the warm clothes that it was with great difficulty that Mrs. Carroll roused them all for bed at ten o'clock.

KATHLEEN THOMPSON NORRIS
Saturday's Child

The smiling Spring comes in rejoicing,
    And surly Winter grimly flies;
Now crystal clear are the falling waters,
    And bonie blue are the sunny skies..
Fresh o'er the mountains breaks forth the morning,
    The ev'ning gilds the ocean's swell;
All creatures joy in the sun's returning,
    And I rejoice in my bonie Bell.

The flowery Spring leads sunny Summer,
    The yellow Autumn presses near;
Then in his turn comes gloomy Winter,
    Till smiling Spring again appear:
Thus seasons dancing, life advancing,
    Old Time and Nature their changes tell;
But never ranging, still unchanging,
    I adore my bonie Bell.

ROBERT BURNS

WELCOME TO OUR NEST

26

This cabin was not his, by the way, having been built several years previously by a couple of miners who had got out a raft of logs at that point for a grub-stake. They had been most hospitable lads, and, after they abandoned it, travelers who knew the route made it an object to arrive there at nightfall. It was very handy, saving them all the time and toil of pitching camp; and it was an unwritten rule that the last man left a neat pile of firewood for the next comer. Rarely a night passed but from half a dozen to a score of men crowded into its shelter.

JACK LONDON
The Man with the Gash

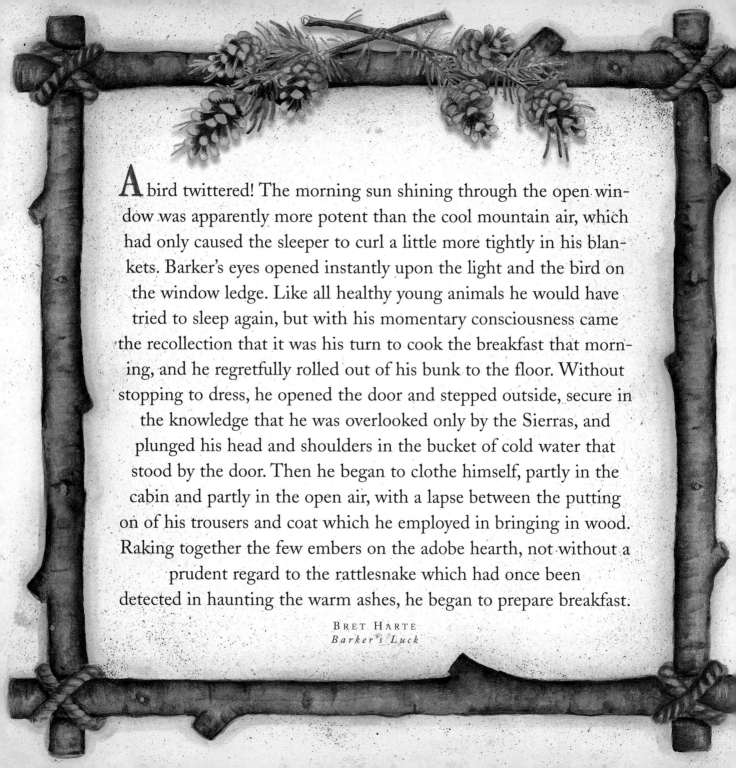

A bird twittered! The morning sun shining through the open window was apparently more potent than the cool mountain air, which had only caused the sleeper to curl a little more tightly in his blankets. Barker's eyes opened instantly upon the light and the bird on the window ledge. Like all healthy young animals he would have tried to sleep again, but with his momentary consciousness came the recollection that it was his turn to cook the breakfast that morning, and he regretfully rolled out of his bunk to the floor. Without stopping to dress, he opened the door and stepped outside, secure in the knowledge that he was overlooked only by the Sierras, and plunged his head and shoulders in the bucket of cold water that stood by the door. Then he began to clothe himself, partly in the cabin and partly in the open air, with a lapse between the putting on of his trousers and coat which he employed in bringing in wood. Raking together the few embers on the adobe hearth, not without a prudent regard to the rattlesnake which had once been detected in haunting the warm ashes, he began to prepare breakfast.

BRET HARTE
Barker's Luck

Give me my
scallop-shell
of quiet...

SIR WALTER RALEIGH

POST CARD

There was a time when meadow, grove, and stream,
The earth, and every common sight,
To me did seem
Appareled in celestial light,
The glory and the freshness of a dream.

WILLIAM WORDSWORTH

29

The heavens declare the glory of God; the skies proclaim the work of his hands. Day after day they pour forth speech; night after night they display knowledge. There is no speech or language where their voice is not heard. Their voice goes out into all the earth, their words to the ends of the world.

THE BOOK OF PSALMS

Stones and trees speak slowly and may take a week to get out a single sentence, and there are few men, unfortunately, with the patience to wait for an oak to finish a thought.

GARRISON KEILLOR

31

THERE'S NO PLACE LIKE THE CABIN.

Full many a glorious morning have I seen
Flatter the mountain-tops with sovereign eye,
Kissing with golden face the meadows green,
Gilding pale streams with heavenly alchemy.

WILLIAM SHAKESPEARE

The cabin of large, peeled, golden oak logs, oiled to preserve them, nestled like a big mushroom on the side of the hill. Above and behind the building the trees arose in a green setting. The roof was stained to their shades. The wide veranda was enclosed in screening, over which wonderful vines climbed in places, and round it grew ferns and deep-wood plants. Inside hung big baskets of wild growth; there was a wide swinging seat, with a back rest, supported by heavy chains. There were chairs and a table of bent saplings and hickory withes. Two full stories the building arose, and the western sun warmed it almost to orange-yellow, while the graceful vines crept toward the roof.

GENE STRATTON-PORTER
The Harvester

From July, 1845, to
September, 1847, I lived
by myself in the forest,
in a fairly good cabin,
plastered and warmly
covered, which I built
myself. There I earned all
I needed, and kept to my
own affairs. During that
time my weekly outlay
was but seven and twenty
cents; and I had an
abundance of all sorts.

HENRY DAVID THOREAU

Hushed in the smoky haze of summer sunset,
When I came home again from far-off places,
How many times I saw my western city
        Dream by her river.

Then for an hour the water wore a mantle
Of tawny gold and mauve and misted turquoise
Under the tall and darkened arches bearing
        Gray, high-flung bridges.

Against the sunset, water-towers and steeples
Flickered with fire up the slope to westward,
And old warehouses poured their purple shadows
        Across the levee.

High over them the black train swept with thunder,
Cleaving the city, leaving far beneath it
Wharf-boats moored beside the old side-wheelers
        Resting in twilight.

SARA TEASDALE
"Sunset"

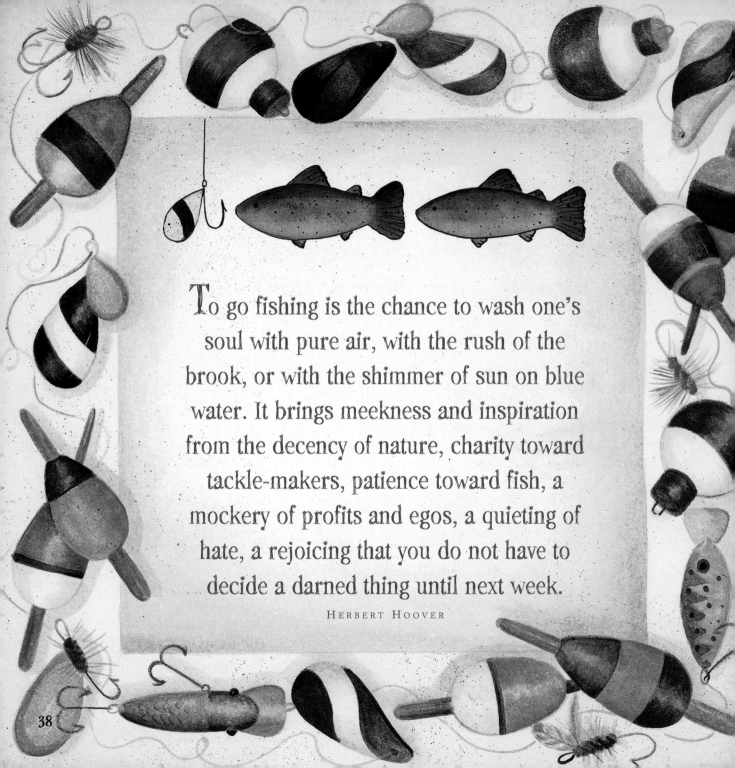

To go fishing is the chance to wash one's soul with pure air, with the rush of the brook, or with the shimmer of sun on blue water. It brings meekness and inspiration from the decency of nature, charity toward tackle-makers, patience toward fish, a mockery of profits and egos, a quieting of hate, a rejoicing that you do not have to decide a darned thing until next week.

HERBERT HOOVER

Why leap the fountains from their cells
Where everlasting Bounty dwells?—
That, while the Creature is sustained,
His God may be adored.

Cliffs, fountains, rivers, seasons, times—
Let all remind the soul of heaven;
Our slack devotion needs them all;
And Faith—so oft of sense the thrall,
While she, by aid of Nature, climbs—
May hope to be forgiven.

WILLIAM WORDSWORTH

Now at the close of this soft summer's day,
Inclined upon the river's flowery side,
I pause to see the sportive fishes play,
And cut with finny oars the sparkling tide.

VALDARNE

I believe in the brook as it wanders from hillside into glade;
I believe in the breeze as it whispers when evening's shadows fade.
I believe in the roar of the river as it dashed from high cascade;
I believe in the cry of the tempest 'mid the thunder's cannonade.

I believe in the light of shining stars, I believe in the sun and the moon;
I believe in the flash of lightning, I believe in the night-bird's croon.
I believe in the faith of the flowers, I believe in the rock and sod,
For in all of these appeareth clear the handiwork of God.

AUTHOR UNKNOWN

A twilight like blue dust sifted into the shallow fold of the thickly wooded hills. It was early October, but a crisping frost had already stamped the maple trees with gold, the Spanish oaks were hung with patches of wine red, the sumac was brilliant in the darkening underbrush. A pattern of wild geese, flying low and unconcerned above the hills, wavered against the serene ashen evening.

LEWIS SINCLAIR

WELCOME
TO THE
CABIN

Who could say the words "Great Smoky Mountains" or "Shenandoah Valley" and not feel an urge, as the naturalist John Muir once put it, to "throw a loaf of bread and a pound of tea in an old sack and jump over the back fence"?

BILL BRYSON
Into the Woods

If one looks long enough at almost anything, looks with absolute attention at a flower, a stone, the bark of a tree, grass, snow, a cloud, something like revelation takes place.

MAY SARTON

43

Must be out-of-doors
enough to get experience of
wholesome reality, as a ballast
to thought and sentiment.
Health requires this
relaxation, this aimless life.

HENRY DAVID THOREAU

Next we slid into the river and had a swim, so as to freshen up and cool off; then we set down on the sandy bottom where the water was about knee deep, and watched the daylight come. Not a sound anywheres—perfectly still—just like the whole world was asleep, only sometimes the bullfrogs a-cluttering, maybe… and you see the mist curl up off of the water, and the east reddens up, and the river, and you make out a log-cabin in the edge of the woods, away on the bank on t'other side of the river…then the nice breeze springs up, and comes fanning you from over there, so cool and fresh and sweet to smell on account of the woods and the flowers… and next you've got the full day, and everything smiling in the sun, and the song-birds just going at it!

MARK TWAIN
Huckleberry Finn

BIG BEAR OUTFITTERS

FISHING GUIDES FOR HIRE

Just reel 'em in!

There is pleasure in the pathless woods,
There is a rapture on the lonely shore,
There is society where none intrudes
By the deep sea, and music in its roar.

GEORGE GORDON

45

A voice of greeting from the wind was sent;
The mists enfolded me with soft white arm;
The birds did sing to lap me in content,
The rivers wove their charms—
And every little daisy in the grass
Did look up in my face, and smile to see me pass!

R. H. STODDARD

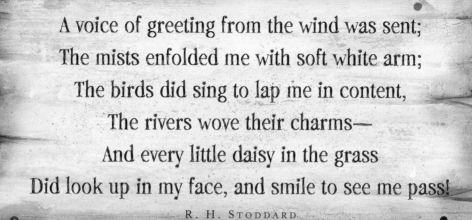

How beautiful the water is!
To me 'tis wondrous fair—
No spot can ever lonely be
If water sparkle there;
It hath a thousand tongues of mirth,
Of grandeur, or delight,
And every heart is gladder made
When water greets the sight.

MRS. E. OAKES SMITH

Climb the mountains and get their good tidings. Nature's peace will flow into you as sunshine flows into trees. The winds will blow their freshness into you, and the storms their energy, while cares will drop off like autumn leaves.

JOHN MUIR